We're Going to the Mountains

WHAT WILL I SEE?

by

Clare Baker-Dukett

illustrations by Tyler Schafle

To order additional copies of this book, contact:
Xlibris
844-714-8691
www.Xlibris.com
Orders@Xlibris.com

ISBN: Softcover   978-1-4500-4281-9
             EBook   979-8-3694-1367-8

Print information available on the last page

Rev. date: 12/16/2023

Dedication

This story is dedicated to our grandchildren who have enjoyed their trips up to the mountains to visit us.

We are going to the mountains.
What will I see?
I see lots of tall pine trees.
I see log cabins in the woods.

There are bears up here.
But, I hope I do not see one.
I see hoof prints of elk or deer.
I hear a fox howling in the night.

We are walking in the woods.
I smell pine trees in the air
and feel the breeze on my face.
It looks like it will rain soon.

I see the rain coming down.
It feels cool and wet on my skin.
I hear thunder in the distance
and see lightning flash in the sky.

We are having a fire in the fireplace.
I feel the heat and see the flames.
I am roasting marshmallows on the fire.
Mmmmm, it tastes sweet and good to eat.

Today we are going to the lake.
I am sitting in a canoe with my
hand dangling in the cold water.
The sun feels good and warm.

I see fish swimming in the water.
We throw food in for them to eat.
I hear birds singing in the trees
and it makes me feel so happy.

Now we are going hiking in the woods.
The trees are so green and the sky so blue.
There is a mountain stream along the trail.
It feels cold and the rushing water sounds loud.

We see a herd of elk in the distance.
I wish we could get closer, but we can't.
They run away when they see us.
Hiking in the woods is fun and exciting.

I love being in the mountains.
I will be sad to say goodbye,
but hope we will be back soon.
Now I know what I will see!!